The Systemic Risk of European Banks during the Financial and Sovereign Debt Crises

Abstract

We propose a hypothetical distress insurance premium (DIP) as a measure of the European banking systemic risk, which integrates the characteristics of bank size, default probability, and interconnectedness. Based on this measure, the systemic risk of European banks reached its height in late 2011 around € 500 billion. We find that the sovereign default spread is the factor driving this heightened risk in the banking sector during the European debt crisis. The methodology can also be used to identify the individual contributions of over 50 major European banks to the systemic risk measure. This approach captures the large contribution of a number of systemically important European banks, but Italian and Spanish banks as a group have notably increased their systemic importance. We also find that bank-specific fundamentals predict the one-year-ahead systemic risk contribution of our sample of banks in an economically meaningful way.

JEL Classification G15, G21, G28.

Keywords: Banking systemic risk, European debt crisis, too-big-to-fail, leverage, interconnectedness, credit default swap, macroprudential regulation.

---

*We benefited from helpful discussions with Viral Acharya, Tobias Adrian, Robert Engle, Paul Glasserman, Michael Gordy, Galina Hale, Philipp Hartmann, Joel Hasbrouck, Erik Heitfield, Jia Li, Nellie Liang, Andrew J. Patton, George Tauchen, Skander Van den Heuvel, David Veredas, and from comments of seminar and conference participants at the Federal Reserve Board, Federal Reserve Bank of San Francisco, University of California Santa Cruz, Duke University, QFE Seminar Series at NYU, Peking University National School of Development, WU Gutmann Center Symposium on Sovereign Credit Risk and Asset Management, 12th Annual Darden International Finance Conference at University of Virginia, FDIC/JFSR 12th Annual Bank Research Conference, G-20 Conference on "Financial Systemic Risk", Bocconi CAREFIN Conference on Banking with Tighter Regulatory Requirements, and the Federal Reserve "Day Ahead" Conference on Financial Markets and Institutions. We would like to thank Clara Vega and Rob Capellini for kindly providing the SRisk and CoVaR data. Michael Carlson and Jason Goldrosen provided excellent research assistance. The analysis and conclusions set forth are those of the authors and not necessarily those of the Board of Governors or its staff.

†Department of Finance, DePaul University, Chicago, IL, USA; phone: 1-703-677-7380; e-mail: lamont.black@gmail.com.

‡Global Financial Institutions Section, Federal Reserve Board of Governors, Washington, D.C., USA; phone: 1-202-452-2213; e-mail: ricardo.correa@frb.gov.

§Risk Analysis Section, Federal Reserve Board of Governors, Washington, D.C., USA; phone: 1-405-517-1038; e-mail: huan6859@gmail.com.

¶PBC School of Finance, Tsinghua University, Beijing, 100083, P. R. China; phone: +86-10-62790655; e-mail:zhouh@pbcsf.tsinghua.edu.cn.

1 Introduction

In late 2011, the European financial system appeared to be on the brink of a major crisis. Investors were faced with the possibility of a Greek default while European leaders wrestled with a fiscal situation that had no clear precedent. As contagion fears spread to Italy and Spain, market participants began to consider the worst-case scenarios. One of the greatest concerns was the systemic risk of the European banking system. If a sovereign default were to lead to a failure of a systemically-important European bank, the resulting financial instability could be disastrous. This type of scenario highlights the need for identifying and understanding the contribution of banks to systemic risk in the financial system.

In this paper, we address the issue by providing a measure of systemic risk for a broad range of European banks. Our systemic risk measure is a summary indicator of market perceived risk that reflects expected default risk of individual banks, risk premia, as well as correlated defaults. Based on our measure of systemic risk, we show that there was significant risk posed by the European banks, which reached its peak in November 2011. At that point in the unfolding of the European sovereign debt crisis, the systemic risk posed by the European banking system and its potential global spillover were clearly main focus of all bank regulators and market participants.

Our analysis builds on the recent literature attempting to measure systemic risk using only publicly available information (see, e.g., Adrian and Brunnermeier (2011), Acharya, Pedersen, Philippon, and Richardson (2010), and Brownlees and Engle (2012), among others). We empirically measure systemic risk as a hypothetical insurance premium to cover distressed losses in the European banking system, based on the inputs of credit default swap (CDS) spreads, equity return correlations, and total liabilities of individual banks. These components capture the main characteristics of systemic risk—default risk, interconnectedness, and bank size (Huang, Zhou, and Zhu, 2009, 2012).[1]

---

[1] For an overview of methodologies in systemic risk analysis, see Bisias, Flood, Lo, and Valavanis (2012). These systemic risk measures are useful complements to balance sheet information–such as the IMF Fi-

1

After developing this measure of systemic risk, we explore the determinants of systemic risk as well as the contributions from individual banks and countries. The ultimate goal is to understand the sources of systemic risk. The main findings provide a number of insights into the nature of European banks' systemic risk and point to important policy implications.

First, the systemic risk indicator for European banks is elevated in the financial crisis and sovereign debt crisis, but the determinants of systemic risk during these periods appear to differ. In 2008 and 2009, the movement in the indicator for European banks reflects spillover effects of the U.S. financial crisis. All banks across the region felt the stress of the failure of Lehman Brothers in 2008. During this stage of the global financial crisis, market perception of the systemic risk of European banks appears to have been mainly driven by the risk premium component. This suggests that the stress was mostly due to heightened risk aversion and liquidity hoarding in the global financial markets.

The elevated systemic risk of European banks during the sovereign debt crisis—reaching its height in 2011—was largely due to increased default risk. Systemic risk quickly increased with the Greek bailout agreement in May 2010 and, as the European sovereign debt crisis unraveled, the systemic risk of European banks rapidly rose to its highest peak in November 2011. Physical default probabilities of European banks rose substantially in the second half of 2011, which points to real solvency risk as a major contributor to systemic risk. This suggests that European banks were faced with real solvency threats from their balance sheets, likely due to their holdings of peripheral European sovereign debt. Systemic risk only began to decline at the end of 2011, which may be attributable to additional liquidity injections from the European Central Bank (ECB).

However, there was another huge run-up in the systemic risk measure in the second quarter of 2012, concerning potential default of a major European country—Spain. Ultimately, the sustained decline of the European banking systemic risk, only occurred after Mario Draghi's "courageous leap" speech in May and "whatever it takes" speech in July, followed

nancial Sector Assessment Program (FSAP)–and supervisors' stress tests based on *confidential* banking information—such as the 2009 Supervisory Capital Assessment Program (SCAP) by the U.S. regulators.

by the announcement of the ECB's nonconventional monetary policy—Outright Monetary Transactions (OMT) in August 2012. At the end of our data sample—January 2013, the European banking systemic risk has roughly returned to the level of May 2010—around the time of the first Greek bailout.

Second, the analysis on the marginal contribution of each bank (or bank group) to the systemic risk indicator suggests that bank size and interconnectedness are very important in determining the systemic importance of individual banks, which is consistent with Tarashev, Borio, and Tsatsaronis (2009b). This result supports the "too-big-to-fail" concern from a macroprudential perspective. The increase in the systemic risk contributions of certain "small" banks can be largely attributed to the deterioration in credit quality (increases in default probability and/or correlation) of these banks.

In our country analysis, we find that the banking systems of certain countries played unique roles during recent periods. For instance, the systemic importance of U.K. banks rose and fell with the global financial crisis, corresponding to their role as global financial centers. In the sovereign debt crisis, the largest increase in contributions to systemic importance has come from the Italian and Spanish banks. This suggests that concerns regarding relatively smaller banks in these southern European countries can still have significant systemic risk implications for the rest of Europe, possibly due to the high correlation or contagion effect. These findings provide empirical support for the European-wide macroprudential regulation regime of systemically important banks and/or groups of banks.

We also demonstrate that bank-specific economic fundamentals do predict the one-year ahead systemic risk contribution of each bank, in an economically meaningful way. For example, firm size and the leverage ratio forecast increases in systemic risk, while short-term funding adequacy and a favorable market valuation ratio forecast decreases in systemic risk. More importantly, Basel capital ratio and implicit government support actually lead to future increases in systemic risk, which suggests that the traditional microprudential regulation regime inadvertently gives banks strong incentives to take on more systemic risk.

Our study is motivated by the euro area's struggle since 2010 with the twin crises of sovereign and financial default. To decouple the vicious cycle of sovereign and financial default contagion, the euro area needs not only a fiscal union and a lender of last resort, but also a banking union with a common resolution regime, deposit insurance, and banking supervision and regulation. Our research contributes to the development of euro-area banking regulation—to monitor euro area-wide financial stability and to supervise the systemically important euro-area banks—as it is underway following a proposal to grant the ECB broad supervisory authority over euro-area banks. For instance, policymakers have debated whether the euro-area banking regulator should be responsible for 6000 banks or only the 25 largest banks. Our results point to something in between—not only the systemically-important largest banks but also the systemically-important banking systems of certain countries.[2] The appropriate macroprudential regulation of the euro area's banks could help secure Europe's need for financial stability.

Our research contributes to the global effort of macroprudential regulation. The global financial crisis of 2007-2009 led international regulators to adopt a system-wide macroprudential approach to bank regulation (see, Borio, 2011, for a summary). The macroprudential perspective of regulation focuses on the soundness of the banking system as a whole and the interlinkages between financial stability and the real economy (see, e.g., Bernanke, Gertler, and Gilchrist, 1998; Adrian and Boyarchenko, 2012; He and Krishnamurthy, 2012). Such an approach has become an overwhelming theme in the policy recommendations by international policy institutions, national stability regulators, and academic researchers (see, Brunnermeier, Crockett, Goodhart, Persaud, and Shin, 2009; Basel Committee on Banking Supervision, 2009; U.S. Congress, 2010, among others). The macro-prudential perspective was first proposed by Crockett (2000) and Borio (2003). In particular, macroprudential

---

[2]Europe traditionally has more of a bank-based financial system than a market-based financial system like the United States, so the systemic importance of individual banks is even greater for financial stability (Allen and Gale, 1995). Also in Europe, the financial and economic integration in recent decades implies that the health of individual European banks has implications for the financial stability of the entire region (Bolton and Jeanne, 2011).

features of the new Basel III accord include additional capital surcharges on systemically-important financial institutions (SIFI's), which is in sharp contrast with the microprudential features of the old Basel I and Basel II accords. Our findings on individual banks' contributions to systemic risk may shed light on the issue of a SIFI capital surcharge for banks around the world.

The remainder of the paper is organized as follows. Section 2 outlines the methodology. Section 3 introduces the data for the major banks in the European banking system along with some descriptive statistics. Section 4 presents empirical results and the final section concludes.

2 Methodology

A consistent framework for systemic risk analysis, as suggested by Borio (2011), should integrate both a time-series aspect of well-defined aggregate systemic risk concept and a cross-section aspect of proper decomposition into each institution's marginal contribution. Our methodology aims to address three important issues. First, the systemic risk indicator measures the risk for a portfolio of heterogeneous banks; second, how to decompose the systemic risk measure into different components relating to risk factors and economic sources; third, the methodology offers an assessment of the contribution of each bank or each group of banks to the systemic risk indicator.

2.1 Constructing the systemic risk indicator

Although there lacks a unified definition of financial systemic risk in an economy (Borio, 2011; Bisias, Flood, Lo, and Valavanis, 2012), an operational systemic risk measure can be constructed as a hypothetical insurance premium against catastrophic losses in a banking system (Huang, Zhou, and Zhu, 2009). To construct this premium, we followed the structural approach of Vasicek (1991) for pricing portfolio credit risk, which is also consistent with the Merton (1974) model of individual firm's default risk. The two key default risk factors, the probability of default (PD) of individual banks and the asset return correlations among banks, are estimated from credit default swap (CDS) spreads and stock return co-movements, respectively.

The one-year *risk-neutral* PDs ($PD_{1,t}$) of individual banks are derived from CDS annual spreads s_t.[3] According to the simplified no-arbitrage condition in Duffie (1999) and Tarashev and Zhu (2008a), the discounted expected quarterly CDS premiums must equal the discounted expected loss-given-default:

$$0.25s_t \sum_{k=1}^{4T} \exp[-(h_{t+0.25k} + r_{t+0.25k})(0.25k)] = LGD_t \int_t^{t+T} h_\tau \exp[-(r_\tau + h_\tau)(\tau - t)]d\tau \quad (1)$$

$$PD_{1,t} = 1 - \exp(-h_t) \quad (2)$$

where LGD_t is the loss-given-default, r_t is the risk-free rate and h_t is the default hazard rate. It is important to point out that the PD implied from a CDS spread is a *risk-neutral* measure, i.e., it reflects not only the *actual* (or physical) default probability but also a risk premium component as well. The risk premium component can be the default risk premium that compensates for uncertain cash flow, a liquidity premium that tends to escalate during a crisis period, or an indirect sovereign default component as in the case of European countries like Greece, Spain, and Italy.[4]

We estimate the asset return correlation by the equity return correlation following Hull and White (2004), because the equity market is very liquid, and can incorporate new information on the relationship between banks much more quickly than the quarterly bank asset data do. Moreover, equity market information is forward-looking while the accounting information on the balance sheet only summarizes the history. On the other hand, the equivalence between asset and equity correlations is exact when the leverage ratio is constant, and

---

[3]CDS spread is considered to be a relative purer measure of credit risk compared to bond or loan spreads (see, Blanco, Brennan, and March, 2005; Forte and Peña, 2009; Norden and Wagner, 2008, among others). Nevertheless, there may still a liquidity component of CDS spread that need to be accounted for (see, e.g., Tang and Yan, 2008)

[4]Puzanova and Düllmann (2013) also take the portfolio approach to measure systemic risk, but using the physical probability of default, and assuming constant LGD and correlations.

is a reasonable approximation in general (Huang, Zhou, and Zhu, 2009) for a short horizon. So the hypothetic insurance contract for our DIP measure covers the default horizon of one quarter.

To ensure the internal consistency of correlation estimates, we match the non-parametric correlation estimates with a proper factor model (Vasicek, 1991; Gordy, 2003). In particular, we assume that the asset return of bank i at time t, $\Delta \log(A_{i,t})$, is driven by C common factors, $M_t = [M_{1,t}, ..., M_{C,t}]'$, and an idiosyncratic factor, $Z_{i,t}$:

$$\Delta \log(A_{i,t}) = B_i M_t + \sqrt{1 - B_i B_i'} \cdot Z_{i,t}, \tag{3}$$

where $B_i = [\beta_{i,1}, ..., \beta_{i,C}]$ is the vector of common factor loading coefficients for bank i (with $i = 1, \cdots, N$), $\beta_{i,c} \in [-1, 1]$ and $\sum_{c=1}^{C} \beta_{i,c}^2 \leq 1$. Without loss of generality, we assume that all the common and idiosyncratic factors are mutually independent and have zero means and unit variances.

To estimate the loading coefficients $B = [B_1; ...; B_N]$, we follow the efficient algorithm proposed by Andersen, Sidenius, and Basu (2003) to solve the following minimization problem:

$$\min \ tr(\Sigma - BB' - F)(\Sigma - BB' - F)' \tag{4}$$

$$\text{s.t. } diag(F) = I - diag(BB'), \tag{5}$$

where tr is the matrix trace operator, i.e., sum of the diagonal elements, Σ is the raw pairwise estimate of the correlation matrix, and the diagonal matrix F ensures that the diagonal of the factor-reduced correlation matrix contains only one's. In general, four to six common factors can explain up to 95% of the total variation in our correlation sample estimates. Meanwhile, the above factor structure can help to increase simulation speed, and ensure positive-semidefiniteness of the correlation matrix as an input for the simulation.

To capture the size effect directly, we use banks' total liabilities as weights in our construction of the systemic risk measure. This is an important feature of our approach, and alternative measures based on value-at-risk (VaR) and expected shortfall (ES) generally do not incorporate this balance-sheet effect directly. Since our "distress insurance premium" measure defines financial distress as the situation in which at least 10% of total liabilities in the banking system go into default, the amount of banks' total liabilities outstanding is a very important input variable to capture the exact economic meaning of too-big-to-fail. For instance, in our sample of 58 European banks, the stress scenario of 10% threshold would mean that at least 2 out of the 8 largest institutions default simultaneously.

Based on the inputs of the key credit risk parameters—risk-neutral PDs, correlations, and liability weights—the systemic risk indicator can be calculated by the simulation approach as described in Huang, Zhou, and Zhu (2009). To compute the indicator, we first construct a hypothetical debt portfolio that consists of total liabilities (deposits, debts and others) of all banks. Let L_i denote the loss of bank i's liability with $i = 1, \cdots, N$; $L = \sum_{i=1}^{N} L_i$ is the total loss of the portfolio. Then the systemic risk of the banking sector, or the distress insurance premium (DIP), is given by the risk-neutral expectation of the loss exceeding a certain threshold level:

$$\text{DIP} = \text{E}^Q \left[L \times 1(L \geq L_{\min}) \right] , \tag{6}$$

where $L_{\min}$ is a minimum loss threshold or "deductible" value. The DIP formula can be easily implemented with Monte Carlo simulation (Huang, Zhou, and Zhu, 2009). Appendix A provides detailed description on the steps to compute DIP.

2.2 Economic composition of systemic risk

In addition to the construction of systemic risk indicator, we also perform several decompositions of the systemic risk into different economic components.

One perspective is to investigate how much of the systemic risk is driven by the movement in *actual* default risk and how much is driven by the movement in *risk premia*, which includes—but is not limited to—default risk premium and the liquidity risk premium. For this purpose, we re-calculate the systemic risk indicator, but using market estimates of the objective or actual default rates rather than the risk-neutral default rates derived from CDS spreads. The corresponding insurance premium against distress losses, on an *actuarial* basis, quantifies the contribution from the expected actual defaults, and the difference between the *market value* (our benchmark result) and the *actuarial* premium quantifies the contribution from risk premia components.

To measure objective or actual PDs, we use expected default frequencies reported by Moody's KMV. This measure of PD should more closely move with changes in banks' balance-sheet risk, such as risk of losses on their holdings of mortgage loans or sovereign debt. On the other hand, our benchmark risk-neutral PD input into the systemic risk construct is backed out from market CDS spreads.

Furthermore, we decompose the risk premium component of the systemic risk measure into three components, the default risk premium in the global market is proxied by the difference between corporate 10-year bond yields of BBB rating over AA rating (see, e.g., Chen, Collin-Dufresne, and Goldstein, 2009), the liquidity risk premium is proxied by the spread of European London interbank offered rates, or LIBOR, over the overnight index swap rate, or OIS (see, e.g., Brunnermeier, 2009), and sovereign risk premium proxied by the spread between Spanish and Italian 10-year sovereign bonds yield and German 10-year Bounds yield. Earlier analysis has shown important differential impacts of default and liquidity risk premium components during different phases of the 2007-2009 global financial crisis (Huang, Zhou, and Zhu, 2012), yet no significant impact of sovereign risk premium has been documented until the European debt crisis since 2010.

When analyzing the default risk of European banks, the response of the sovereign government and/or international institutions to banking distress must be considered. If market participants anticipate a European bank bailout by the its home country or European authority, the risk of the bank's debt will be priced accordingly. Therefore, market prices are not always a good indicator of bank risk when future government intervention is a possibility.

To address this issue, we also estimate banks' risk-neutral PDs from CDS spreads on subordinated debt. Historically, bailouts of European banks have included the bailout of investors in the banks' senior debt, but not the subordinated debt (Moody's Investors Service, 2009). Therefore, CDS spreads on subordinated debt are less subject to the bias of perceived government support. Based on these spreads, we construct an alternative systemic risk indicator that can be compared to the benchmark indicator. Therefore, the difference between the systemic risk measure based on CDS on senior unsecured debt and subordinated debt may provide a crude proxy for market assessment of implicit government support of banks.

2.3   Systemic importance of individual banks

For the purpose of macroprudential regulation, it is important not only to monitor the economy-wide systemic risk, but also to understand each bank's contributions to the aggregate systemic risk. Whereas the macroprudential approach focuses on the risk of the financial system as a whole, in the end regulatory and policy measures are implemented at the level of individual banks. A proper decomposition as described below allows a systemic risk regulator to easily link the regulatory burden to risk contributions of individual banks (Tarashev, Borio, and Tsatsaronis, 2009a).

Following Kurth and Tasche (2003) and Glasserman (2005), for standard measures of risk, including expected shortfall and distress insurance premium proposed here, the total risk can be properly decomposed into a sum of marginal risk contributions. Each marginal risk contribution is the expected loss from that sub-portfolio, when the full portfolio experiences a large loss. In particular, if we define L as the loss variable for the whole portfolio as earlier, and L_i as the loss variable for a sub-portfolio, the marginal contribution to our systemic risk indicator, the distress insurance premium (DIP), can be characterized by

$$\mathrm{E}^Q[L_i \times 1(L \geq L_{\min})] \tag{7}$$

The additive property of the decomposition results, i.e., the systemic risk of a portfolio equals the marginal contribution from each sub-portfolio, is important for operational purpose.

One important alternative to our DIP measure is the CoVaR method proposed by Adrian and Brunnermeier (2011). CoVaR looks at the VaR of the portfolio conditional on the VaR of an individual institution, defined as

$$\text{Prob}\left(r_m \leq \text{CoVaR}_i^{q,p} | r_i = \text{VaR}_i^p\right) = q$$

where r_i is the market-valued asset return of institution i, and r_m is the return of the portfolio, computed as the average of the r_i's weighted by the lagged market-value assets of the institutions in the portfolio. Then Adrian and Brunnermeier (2011) measure institution i's contribution to the systemic risk by ΔCoVaR, defined as

$$\Delta\text{CoVaR}_i^q = \text{CoVaR}_i^{q,q} - \text{CoVaR}_i^{q,0.5}$$

An important concern of CoVaR, or VaR-based measure in general, is that it may not appropriately aggregate the systemic risk contributions of individual institutions.

Another alternative is the MES proposed by Acharya, Pedersen, Philippon, and Richardson (2010). MES looks at the expected loss of each institution conditional on the whole portfolio performing poorly:

$$\text{MES}_i^q \equiv \text{E}\left(r_i | r_m \leq \text{VaR}_m^q\right)$$

where r_i and r_m are the equity returns of institution i and the portfolio.

Based on MES, Brownlees and Engle (2012) and Acharya, Engle, and Richardson (2012) propose another systemic risk measure, called SRISK, which explicitly takes into account the size of a financial institution. The SRISK for institution i is defined as:

$$\begin{aligned} \text{SRISK}_i \;&=\; max[0, E(\text{Capital Shortfall}_i | \text{Systemic Crisis})] \\ &=\; max[0, E(k\,\text{Asset}_i - \text{Equity}_i | \text{Systemic Crisis})] \end{aligned}$$

where k is the prudential equity/asset ratio. Then institution i's contribution to the aggregate SRISK in percentage is given by

$$\text{SRISK\%}_i \;=\; \frac{\text{SRISK}_i}{\sum_{i=1}^{N} \text{SRISK}_i}.$$

There are several differences between DIP and CoVaR, MES or SRISK.

First, conceptually, DIP is a risk-neutral pricing measure that is derived from both CDS and equity market data, while MES, SRISK and CoVaR are objective distribution-based statistical measures that rely mostly on equity return information. So the latter are pure measure of the physical systemic risk, while DIP also contains various risk premium components.

Second, DIP, MES and SRISK measure each institution's loss when the system is in distress, while CoVaR measures the system loss conditional on each institution being in distress.

Third, MES and SRISK calculate the institution loss when the systemic loss has been realized while DIP is the ex ante loss, taking into account the probability of the systemic risk. So MES and SRISK can be much higher in magnitude than DIP.

Fourth, neither CoVaR nor MES incorporates institution size as an *ex ante* input in constructing the systemic risk indicator, while DIP and SRISK do.

As the above concepts measure the systemic risk from different angles, they can provide complementary information in the real-time supervisory monitoring of the financial systemic risk.

3 Data summary and descriptive analysis

In July 2011, the European Banking Authority (EBA) released the results of their stress tests for a broad range of 90 European banks, which included large banks from countries around Europe, such as banks from Austria, Belgium, Denmark, France, Germany, Greece, Ireland, Italy, Luxembourg, the Netherlands, Norway, Portugal, Spain, Sweden, and the United Kingdom. This group of banks is the starting point of our sample. To the list of banks that participated in the EBA stress test, we add the two large systemically important institutions from Switzerland (UBS and Credit Suisse) and a few others not included in the stress test. Our initial raw sample is composed of close to 100 European banks. We then apply the following data availability criteria for each bank: (i) a minimum number of 200 valid observations of daily CDS spreads since January 1, 2005; (ii) publicly available equity prices since January 1, 2003; and (iii) a minimum number of 20 valid observations of monthly EDFs since January 2005. This results in a final sample of 58 banks.[5]

Our sample data cover the period from January 2001 to January 2013, allowing us to track the evolution of European banks from before the financial crisis through the still evolving sovereign debt crisis. For bank balance sheet data, including total equity and liabilities, we use Datastream. Market variables, including CDS spreads and EDFs, are used at a higher frequency. We retrieve weekly CDS spreads and recovery rates from Markit.[6] EDFs of individual banks are provided by Moody's KMV. EDF is a market product that estimates expected one-year (physical) default rates of individual firms based on their balance sheet information and equity price data. The method is based on the Merton (1974) framework and explained in detail in Crosbie and Bohn (2002). In this study, we assume that EDFs track closely physical expectations of default. See Appendix B for details on all the data that we use in this paper.

Table 1 reports some basic descriptive statistics about the banks in our sample. In this table, we show figures from the banks' balance sheets and market prices according to eight groupings of banks by home country. The first set of columns in Table 1 report the "group" for each bank and the second column lists the home countries in each group.

For the larger European countries including France (FR), Germany (GE), Great Britain (GB) and Switzerland (SZ), the group is the set of banks within a single country (e.g.,

---

[5]The total assets of the 58 banks in our data sample is about 58% of the whole European banking sector asset. Also the frequency for the EDF data gradually increased from monthly to daily for the sample banks over the sample period.

[6]We used the last available daily observation in each week. Recovery rates are reported by market participants who contribute quotes of CDS spreads.

French banks and German banks). Smaller countries are combined into groups, such as the group for Austria (AS), Belgium (BE), Luxembourg (LX), and the Netherlands (NE) and the group for Denmark (DE), Norway (NO), and Sweden (SW). For the "peripheral" European countries, we combine Italy (IT) and Spain (SP) and also Greece (GR), Ireland (IR) and Portugal (PO). We also use these groupings for some of our later analysis, such as the calculation of within-group correlations.

The summary statistics of total equities, total liabilities, CDS spreads and EDFs (expected default frequencies) in Table 1 provide some context for the subsequent analysis. The Total Equity and Total Liability columns are the sum of the book value equity and liabilities of the banks in each group. As can be seen, these values for the British and the French banks are larger than those of any other European country. The amount of liabilities are particularly important in our measure of systemic risk as it relates to the concept of size or too-big-to-fail, which dominates expected losses during distress times.

The CDS spreads and EDFs for each group of banks are reported as averages during three periods. Period 1 is the pre-crisis period, which covers January 1, 2005 to August 8, 2007, the day before BNP Paribas froze redemption on several of its hedge funds. Period 2 is the financial crisis and recovery period, spanning August 9, 2007 to May 1, 2010, the day before the Greek government accepted the € 110 billion EU-IMF support package. And finally, period 3 is the sovereign debt crisis, which begins on May 2, 2010 and goes through the end of our sample in January 2013. The key comparisons from this table are across countries and over time. As can be seen, the CDS spreads for Italian and Spanish banks were low relative to many of the large European countries during the pre-sovereign debt crisis period. The dramatic rise in CDS spreads during the sovereign debt crisis in period 3 is seen for all countries, but especially for the banks in the peripheral countries, including Spain and Italy.

Figure 1 plots the time variation in key credit risk variables: PDs, recovery rates, and correlations. We compute the historical correlations between the banks from equity price data (which start from January 2003) provided by Datastream.

The *risk-neutral* PDs (top-left panel) are derived from the CDS spreads and recovery rates. The weighted averages (weighted by the size of bank liabilities) are not much different from median CDS spreads in most of the sample period. They were very low (a few basis points) before July 2007. With the developments of the global financial crisis, risk-neutral PDs of European banks increased quickly and the average PD reached a peak of 5% in October 2008, shortly after the failure of Lehman Brothers. The risk-neutral PD fell in 2009, after the height of the financial crisis, but began increasing again in 2010. The average risk-neutral PD continued to rise in 2011, reaching levels during the European sovereign crisis that exceeded the levels in the global financial crisis. This comparison with the financial crisis provides the first indication of major systemic risk in the European banking system during the European sovereign debt crisis—the default risk for European banks in 2011 had reached a historical high. The min-max range of the CDS spreads also points to the substantial differences across European banks in term of credit quality. The European banks with the greatest solvency risk had reached PDs of over 50%.

The physical measure of PDs of European banks (top-right panel), as measured using EDFs, were also at very low levels prior to 2007. However, this measure did not increase much during the global financial crisis and only began to approach the levels of risk-neutral PD during 2011. This increase in EDFs during the sovereign crisis is consistent with the deterioration in macroeconomic prospects in most European economies. Economic growth slowed down substantially and turned negative. These developments generated concerns about the asset quality of banks in the region and therefore EDFs went up. In addition, as European countries were hit by the sovereign crisis in different degrees, the changes in EDFs also showed substantial cross-sectional differences. The high skewness of the EDF data in Period 3 on Table 1, as proxied by the difference between each group mean and whole sample medium, shows that the impact of the crisis was felt the strongest among the Greek, Irish and Portuguese banks, but very little by the Danish, Norwegian and Swedish banks.

Recovery rates (lower-left panel) are *ex ante* measures, i.e., expected recovery rates when

CDS contracts are priced, and hence can differ substantially from the *ex post* observations of a handful default events during our sample period. In addition, whereas we allow for time-varying recovery rates, they exhibit only small variation (between 36 and 43%) during the sample period.[7]

The other key credit risk factor, the asset return correlation (lower-right panel), shows small variation over time but large cross-sectional differences. Average correlations were below 40% during the period just prior to the financial crisis and then began to rise above 40% in 2008. Interestingly, average correlations for European banks have been somewhat lower during the sovereign crisis relative to the financial crisis. This may be due to the common response of European banks to U.S. news during the financial crisis but the heterogeneous response to news coming from specific European countries during the sovereign crisis.

Figure 2 shows the correlation estimates for pairwise correlations and within-group correlations. The equity correlation data begin one year prior to our main sample so that correlations can be calculated over a rolling one-year window. The upper panel plots the averages of pairwise correlations (based on equity return movements) for three categories: for any two banks from the sample (All), for any two banks from the same group (Within), and for any two banks from different groups (Cross). The higher dashed line shows that banks from the same country typically have much higher pairwise correlations than those from different countries. Over time, the pairwise correlations can be as low as 20% and as high as 60%. These differences in pairwise correlations point to the potential bias if the correlation matrix is assumed to be homogeneous.[8]

The lower panel of Figure 2 plots the within-group average correlations for each of the

_____

[7]The raw recovery rate data have a significant sparseness problem, in that a large portion of CDS quotes come without the corresponding recovery rates. Therefore, in this paper we use the HP-filtered recovery rates to reflect the time variation in recovery rates, and at the same time to avoid noisy movements in average recovery rates due to data reporting problems.

[8]A latent-factor analysis shows that the explanatory power of a single-factor model can sometimes drop to 50%. For the portfolio of heterogeneous European banks, it usually takes at least four factors to account for 90% of the cross-sectional variation in pairwise correlations during the years prior to the global financial crisis. Details of these latent-factor analysis are available upon request.

8 groups studied in this paper. During the sovereign crisis, the within-group correlations appear to be highest for Swiss banks as well as the Italian and Spanish banks. In contrast, the German banks have a very low within-group correlation, consistent with the more limited concerns about the German banks.

Table 2 also suggests that the key credit risk factors tend to comove with each other. Not surprisingly, risk-neutral and physical PD measures are highly correlated, suggesting that the underlying credit quality of a bank has an important impact on the credit protection cost. PDs and correlations are also positively correlated, confirming the conventional view that when systemic risk is higher, not only the default risks of individual firms increase but they also tend to move together. Lastly, there is a slightly negative relationship between PDs and recovery rates when computed as the average of bank-specific bivariate correlations. This is consistent with the findings in Altman and Kishore (1996) that recovery rates tend to be lower when credit condition deteriorates (procyclical). Recovery rates also tend to have a negative correlation with the other factors when computed as an average bank-specific correlation.

4 Empirical findings

We apply the methodology described in Section 2 and examine the systemic risk in the European banking system. We first consider the magnitude and determinants of systemic risk, including the role of the risk premium, and then identify the contribution of individual banks to the aggregate indicator of systemic risk and relate these systemic importance of individual banks to their firm-specific economic fundamentals.

4.1 The magnitude and determinants of systemic risk

Figure 3 plots the systemic risk indicator for the European banking system. As explained in Section 2 on the methodology, our systemic risk indicator can be interpreted as a "distress insurance premium", in which financial distress is defined as the situation in which at least

10% of total liabilities in the banking system go into default or at least two out of the largest eight banks default simultaneously. This insurance cost is represented as the premium rate (unit price in percentages) in the upper panel and in Euro amount (€ billions) in the lower panel.

As can be seen immediately in Figure 3, the systemic risk of European banks reached its highest level in late 2011 during the sovereign debt crisis. This points to the severity of the situation facing European leaders as they attempted to defuse the potential disaster of the Greek debt situation. To focus on the two separate crises, we also provide separate expanded figures. Figure 4 shows the systemic risk indicator during the period of the financial crisis, including major dates during the financial crisis such as the freezing of BNP Paribas funds and the failure of Lehman brothers. Figure 5 shows the results with a focus on the period of the sovereign debt crisis in Europe, with a number of dates beginning with the Greek government's acceptance of the € 110 billion EU-IMF support package on May 2, 2010.

The systemic risk indicator for European banks was very low at the beginning of the global financial crisis, shown most clearly in Figure 4. For a long period before BNP Paribas froze three funds due to the subprime problem on August 9, 2007, the aggregate distress insurance premium for the list of 58 European banks was merely several basis points (or less than € 10 billion). The indicator then moved up significantly, reaching the first major peak when Bear Stearns was acquired by JP Morgan on March 16, 2008 (Figure 4). The situation then improved significantly in April-May 2008 owing to strong intervention by major central banks.[9] Things worsened dramatically in September 2008 with the failure of Lehman Brothers. Market panic and increasing risk aversion pushed up the price of insurance against distress in the banking sector, and European banks were not spared. The crisis also hit the real sector, both in the United States and Europe: unemployment went up and forecasts of economic growth were substantially revised downward. The distress insurance

---

[9]The movement of the distress insurance premium for European banks during the global financial crisis is quite similar to that for major US banks as studied in Huang, Zhou, and Zhu (2009), suggesting a possible spillover effect from the global market. This will be further addressed in Section 4.2.

premium for European banks hiked up and hovered in the range of 100 basis points (or €240 billion). The situation didn't improve until late March 2009. In particular, the adoption of unconventional policies, the announcement of a round of stress tests of systemic banks—first in the United States and then in Europe—and strengthened cross-border coordination among policy institutions helped calm the market.

Figure 5 shows the dramatic increase in the systemic risk indicator for European banks during the sovereign debt crisis. Although the indicator had fallen to relatively low levels by the end of 2009, as markets began to stabilize following the global financial crisis, the indicator jumped up in May of 2010 when Greece signed a bailout agreement with the EU and IMF. This appears to have been somewhat of a "new norm" through mid-2011, but, at this point, the crisis reached a new stage. In the summer of 2011, markets began to have significant concerns about the contagion of a Greek default spreading to other European countries. Italy and Spain appeared to be possible dominoes in the next stage of the sovereign crisis. French banks began to show signs of liquidity strains due to their exposure to the sovereign debt of these countries and the withdrawal of funds by U.S. money market mutual funds. As the fears grew, European leaders attempted to halt the downward spiral by issuing greater commitments to financial firewalls, such as expansions to the European Financial Stability Fund (EFSF). Ultimately, our systemic risk indicator reached its peak in November 2011. This appears to be the heart of the sovereign debt crisis, just before the ECB expanded its liquidity provision through a dollar-swap line with the U.S. Federal Reserve and the first of its 3-year Long-Term Refinancing Operations (LTRO) for European banks. There was another run-up in the systemic risk measure in the second quarter of 2012, concerning potential default of Spain. Ultimately, the sustained decline of the European banking systemic risk, only occurred after Mario Draghi's "courageous leap" and "whatever it takes" speeches around June and July, followed by ECB's nonconventional Outright Monetary Transactions (OMT) program launched in August 2012.

One challenge in using CDS spreads to estimate PDs is that CDS spreads may reflect perceptions about the likelihood of government intervention. If market participants expect a bank to be bailed out, they will reduce the price of insuring the bank's debt against default. As a first step to address this possible bias, we have also computed the risk-neutral PDs using CDS spreads on banks' subordinated debt. Subordinated debt holders are less likely to be paid off in a bank bailout, so the CDS spreads should be less influenced by implicit government support.

Figure 6 shows the systemic risk measure based on subordinated debt, with the indicator based on senior debt provided for comparison. As expected, the subordinated debt indicator is higher than the senior debt indicator, which points to greater levels of systemic risk apart from government support.[10] It should be noted that government support reduces the likelihood of bank default, which reduces banks' systemic risk, but during a fiscal crisis this is not the end of the story. Part of the systemic risk posed by the European banking system during the sovereign debt crisis was this very issue. If the sovereign governments were forced to bail out their banks, this would greatly increase their fiscal burden, which would then feedback into the concerns about the sustainability of their sovereign funding.

Table 3 examines the determinants of the systemic risk indicator. The level of risk-neutral PDs is a dominant factor in determining the systemic risk, explaining alone 93% of the variation in the systemic risk indicator (Regression 1). On average, a one-percentage-point increase in average PD raises the systemic risk indicator by 17 basis points. The level of correlation also matters, but to a lesser degree and its impact is largely dissipated once PD is included. This is perhaps due to the strong relationship between PD and correlation for the sample banking group during this special time period. In addition, the recovery rate has the expected negative sign in the multivariate regressions, as higher recovery rates reduce the ultimate losses for a given default scenario.

Interestingly, the heterogeneity in PDs across banks has an additional role in explaining

---

[10]The higher indicator for subordinated debt could also be due to the greater credit risk in subordinated debt due simply to subordination. We are not able to separate these two effects, although during the European debt crisis they are essentially the same.

the movement in the systemic risk indicator (as shown in the bottom of Table 3). The dispersion in PDs across the 58 banks has a significantly negative effect on the systemic risk indicator.[11] This partly supports our view that incorporating heterogeneity in PDs is important in measuring the system risk indicator. It also suggests that greater dispersion of PDs tends to lower the probability of default clustering and by extension reduce the cost of protection against distressed losses. This has interesting implications for models of systemic risk based on the number of banks failing rather than the size of banks that fail, as in "too many to fail" (Acharya, 2009).

The results have two important implications for bank supervisors. First, given the predominant role of average PDs in determining the systemic risk, a first-order approximation of the systemic risk indicator could use the weighted average of PDs (or CDS spreads). This can be confirmed by comparing the similar trend in average PDs (the upper-left panel in Figure 1) and the distress insurance premium (Figure 3). The large role of PDs suggests that microprudential supervision, which focuses on PD, is an important input into macroprudential supervision. Second, the average PD is a decent approximation but it is not sufficient in reflecting the changes in the systemic risk. Correlations and heterogeneity in PDs also matter, as emphasized in a macroprudential perspective.

4.2 The role of risk premium

As mentioned in Section 2, the probabilities of default (PDs) implied by CDS spreads are a risk-neutral measure and include information not only on expected actual default losses of the banking system but also on default risk premium and liquidity risk premium components. It has been argued that, during a general crisis, the risk premium component could be the dominant factor in determining CDS spreads (see, e.g., Kim, Loretan, and Remolona, 2009). Given that the benchmark systemic risk indicator is based on risk-neutral measures, we can

---

[11]Dispersion is represented as the standard deviation of the variable of interest for the sample banks at each particular point in time. The correlation coefficient for a particular bank is defined as the average pairwise correlation between this bank and other banks.

assess how much of its movement is driven by market sentiments (change in attitudes toward default risk and liquidity risk) and how much is attributable to the change in the "pure" credit quality (or actual potential default loss) of the banks. This part of the analysis builds on the the upper panels in Figure 1 that provided an initial perspective on the aggregate trends in these two measures of default likelihood for European banks.

Figure 7 shows the discrepancies between the two measures of probability of default for the banks within each group (based on home country). Each of the eight panels provides a comparison of the risk-neutral PDs implied from CDS spreads with the physical (or actual) PDs estimated by Moody's KMV—EDF, the estimates of the PDs perceived by the market. As can be clearly seen, the significant increase in risk-neutral PDs in October 2008 was primarily driven by the heightened risk premium component. In other words, the average risk-neutral PDs increased significantly, but physical PDs did not increase nearly as much. The difference is explained by an increased risk premium.

In 2011, both PD measures increased sharply, reflecting the fact that the European sovereign debt crisis placed the European banks in a full-fledged economic crisis. The sovereign debt crisis is a crisis of European origin, so the "pure" credit quality of European banks, especially as it relates to losses on sovereign debt, is likely much greater during this period relative to the global financial crisis. While the loss of confidence remained as the main concern in the financial market, the spillover to the real sector led to the drop in global demand and caused significant downward revisions in forecasts of macroeconomic performance in Europe. The deterioration in the real economy imposed heavy pressure on the banking system. As a result, market expectations on the health of European banks were revised down even further.

The failure probability based on EDFs increased most remarkably in 2011 for banks in core European countries, such as France and Germany. In contrast, the systemic risk for the Italian and Spanish banks appears to have been driven primarily by the risk premium. These results suggest that some core European banks may have had higher CDS premiums due to actual risk of losses on sovereign holdings (e.g., French banks), whereas some peripheral banks were pressured by investors due to a shift in market sentiment (e.g., Italian banks).

If we use the physical PD measure (EDF) as the input, we can calculate an alternative systemic risk indicator which assumes that all risk premium components are zeros. In other words, the new indicator reflects an insurance premium on an *actuarial* basis, without compensation for bearing the uncertainty in payoff. Figure 8 plots the EDF-based systemic indicator for the full sample period, along with the benchmark CDS-based indicator for comparison.

The level and trend of the EDF-based indicator clearly differs from the benchmark result. First, the EDF-based indicator is lower, which provides strong evidence on the resilience of European banks during the crisis. In the worst time (late 2011), the EDF-based indicator less than 105 basis points (or € 270 billion), which was only a small-fraction of the CDS-based indicator. This suggests that, during a crisis period, the bailout cost of a market-based solution tends to be larger than that justified by an objective assessment of the default losses, because of risk aversion and liquidity dry-up. Second, CDS spreads (main drivers of risk premium) typically lead bank equity prices (main drivers of EDFs) at the early stages of the crisis. The EDF-based indicator shows that actual credit problem did not deteriorate until the summer of 2011. This provides a different picture from the benchmark case with risk-neutral PD measure, which began increasing in 2010.[12]

Based on the rapid increase of the EDF-based indicator in 2011, it appears that physical default risk was a greater contributor to the systemic risk of European banks during the sovereign debt crisis. The elevated systemic risk for European banks in 2008 is driven primarily by rising risk premia due to a spillover effect from the global financial crisis. This is not the full story for the sovereign debt crisis. Since the second half of 2011, both actual default risk and risk premia (or risk aversion) have risen substantially as the sovereign debt crisis turned into a real economic recession for Europe.

---

[12]Indeed, the decoupling between CDS-implied PDs and EDFs is a phenomenon that characterizes not only European banks, but also U.S. banks studied in Huang, Zhou, and Zhu (2012).

In addition, we also run a regression analysis that examines the impact of physical default rates and risk premium factors on the systemic risk indicator. In Table 4, physical default risk (or objective default rates) is proxied by average distance-to-default (DTD) of sample banks, the corporate default risk premium in the European market is proxied by the difference between BBB- and AA-rated corporate 10-year bond yields (see Chen, Collin-Dufresne, and Goldstein, 2009), the liquidity risk premium in the global market is proxied by the European LIBOR-OIS spread (see Brunnermeier, 2009), and the sovereign risk premium, as we propose, is measured by the spread between Spanish and Italian 10-year sovereign bond yields and 10-year German Bunds. We choose DTD, instead of EDF, to proxy physical default risk in this regression analysis, because DTD reveals the pure information from the current stock market. EDF uses DTD as the major input, but it also relies on a mapping based on historical default events to translate DTD to default probabilities.

As shown in the table, the sovereign risk premium explains most of the variation in the systemic risk indicator. In univariate regressions, sovereign risk premium explains 90% of the total systemic risk variation, much higher than credit risk premium (11%) and liquidity risk premium (20%) and even higher than the DTD—physical default risk (59%). Furthermore, in the multivariate joint regression, the total explaining power increases to 94% with the default risk premium being driven to be statistically insignificant.

Figure 9 plots the contribution effect of actual default risk, default risk premium, liquidity risk premium, and sovereign risk premium, according to the multivariate joint regression in Table 4. As can be seen, the liquidity risk premium was the significant contributor to the systemic risk of European banks during the financial crisis, especially in late 2008. Its contribution also rose in late 2011. The two surges in its contribution match the two peaks of the DIP measure. This observation is consistent with the liquidity dry-up feature of the recent crisis, and reflects the associated market concerns.

However, for the sovereign debt crisis in 2010 and 2011, the primary contributor has been the sovereign risk premium. The increase in the spread between Spanish and Italian sovereign bond yields and German yields has been the main driver in the run-up in systemic risk for European banks, especially in late 2011 and the summer of 2012. This shows that our measure of systemic risk as a distress insurance premium is relatively successful at capturing the main risk to bank solvency during the sovereign debt crisis.

In comparison, the contribution from the physical stress, DTD, to DIP remained significant throughout our sample, and steadily increased from financial crisis to sovereign debt crisis, showing that prolonged financial crisis weakened the economic fundamental, making physical stress more prominent.

Lastly, as insignificant in the multivariate joint regression in Table 4, the default risk premium (Bbb-Aa) does not show up visibly in Figure 9. The insignificance is perhaps due to the strong European government intervention during the recent financial crisis, so that the market is not overly concerned about charging a premium for the default risk.

4.3   The contributions of individual banks to systemic risk

The other natural question is the institutional sources of vulnerabilities, i.e., which banks are systemically more important or contribute the most to the increased vulnerability? Using the methodology described in Section 2, we are able to provide an answer to this question.

We first calculate the marginal contributions of each group of banks to the systemic risk indicator, both in level terms and in percentage terms. Table 5 lists the 58 banks in our sample and provides further details on the marginal contribution of each bank at five dates: (i) August 9, 2007: the day that BNP Paribas froze redemption on several of its hedge funds; (ii) March 7, 2009: the highest peak of the systemic risk indicator during the financial crisis; (iii) May 2, 2010: the Greek government accepts the EU-IMF support package; (iv) November 26, 2011: the highest peak of the systemic risk indicator during the sovereign debt crisis; and (v) January 24, 2013: the lowest point of the systemic risk indicator at the end of our sample period. The last column lists bank equity in 2011 and its difference with 2007 in parentheses.

Several observations are worthy of special remark. First, the biggest contributors to the systemic risk, or the systemically important banks, often coincide with the biggest banks in the region. One example is Royal Bank of Scotland, the bank in our sample with the largest amount of total liabilities. Although its CDS spread (or implied PD) is relatively low compared to the other banks, its contribution to the systemic risk has always been one of the highest. By contrast, some banks with very high CDS spreads, but smaller in size (e.g., the Spanish cajas), are generally not systemically important as individual banks for the European region based on marginal contribution analysis. Second, one can compare the systemic risk contribution of each bank with its equity capital position to judge the source of vulnerability of the banking system. It is clear that, at the beginning phase of the financial crisis, German and British banks were most affected in that they explained the majority of the increase in the systemic risk. For instance, the risk contribution of Deutsche Bank in November 2011 was almost the same as its equity capital as of 2011. Since the failure of Lehman Brothers, other European banks were almost all severely hit. For instance, the systemic risk contribution of Lloyd's of London was as high as € 24 billion on March 7, 2009 and € 23 billion on November 26, 2011, over one-third of its equity capital as of 2011. Were the risk materialized, this category of banks are most likely to face difficulty in raising fresh equity from the market and therefore warrant special attention from systemic risk monitors or regulators.

Figure 10 shows the time series of this marginal contribution of each group of banks by group. In relative terms, the marginal contribution of each group of banks were quite stable prior to the global financial crisis. French banks contributed the most to systemic risk. Interestingly, the systemic contribution of banks in Germany and the U.K. increased the most dramatically in 2006, just prior to the onset of the financial crisis. However, in 2008, the relative contribution of German and U.K. banks decreased substantially. This corresponded to a relative increase in the contributions of other European countries.

The systemic risk contribution of some of the European countries changed substantially between the financial crisis and the sovereign debt crisis. In particular, the systemic risk contribution of Italian and Spanish banks increased the most during the sovereign debt crisis period. While the contribution of German banks remained low, the contribution of U.K. somewhat increased again in the later part of the sample. By country, the largest contributors of banks to the systemic risk are the Italian, Spanish and U.K. banks. It is interesting to note that Spanish and Italian banks were very minor players during the global financial crisis, likely due to their more traditional business models of local lending and local deposit-taking. In contrast, these banks have now become major players in the unfolding of the sovereign debt crisis. Perhaps due to their local risk concentration and their holdings of sovereign debt, they pose significant systemic risk for the current situation in Europe.

Table 6 examines the determinants of marginal contribution to the systemic risk for each bank, using an OLS regression on the panel data. To control for bias, we use clustered standard errors grouped by banks as suggested by Peterson (2009). The first regression shows that weight, or the size effect, is the primary factor in determining marginal contributions both in level and in relative terms. This is not surprising, given the conventional "too-big-to-fail" concern and the fact that bigger banks often have stronger inter-linkage with the rest of the banking system. Interestingly, equity correlations are a greater determinant of a European bank's contribution to systemic risk than a bank's probability of default. This supports the claim that interconnectedness should be a factor in determining banks status as globally systemically-important financial institutions (G-SIFI's). It also supports the view for distinguishing between micro- and macro-prudential perspectives of banking regulation, i.e., the failure of individual banks does not contribute significantly to the increase in systemic risk. The second and third regressions suggest that there are significant interactive effects. Adding interactive terms between weight and PD or correlation have additional and significant explanatory power, indicating that there is a significantly nonlinear contribution of the three systemic risk inputs—that is, PD, correlation, and size. Overall, the results suggest that the marginal contribution is the highest for high-weight (i.e. large) banks which observe increases in PDs or correlations.

The nonlinear effect documented in Table 6 is clearer in a hypothetical calibration exercise examining the relationship between the systemic contribution based on our indicator and an institution's size (total liability), (risk-neutral) default probability, and (average) historical correlation, as shown in Figure 11. The relationship looks nonlinear with respect to size and, convex with respect to PD and correlation. For a few relatively large banks, they contribute a lot more to the systemic risk than the rest of smaller banks. An intuitive reason is that, when a bank is too big, its failure is considered a systemic failure by definition. This consideration may indicate a desirable maximum size of the large complex financial institutions, which, by limiting the systemic risk, could provide a social benefit. The relationship between systemic importance and PD or correlation shows a similar nonlinear pattern but is less dramatic. In other words, systemic importance is a joint effect of an institution's size, PD and correlation with other banks, and is highly nonlinear.

As discussed earlier, our marginal contribution measure is an alternative measure related to the SRisk measure suggested by Brownlees and Engle (2012) and Acharya, Engle, and Richardson (2012), and the ΔCoVaR measure suggested by Adrian and Brunnermeier (2011). SRisk is designed to measure the expected capital shortfall associated with a financial institution when the whole financial system is in crisis, and ΔCoVaR calculates the VaR of the financial system when a financial institution is in distress. The results for our DIP measure and these other two measures are shown in Table 7.[13] The first group of columns compares the values for each bank as of March 7, 2009 during the financial crisis and the second group of columns compares the values on November 26, 2011 during the sovereign debt crisis. We sort the table by DIP on November 26, 2011, and we are looking at how this DIP measure compares to the G-SIFI list published by the Financial Stability Board (FSB) on November 4, 2011. It is interesting to see that DIP is a pretty accurate predictor of G-SIFI's. Moreover, there are some differences: Intesa Sanpaolo in Italy and BBVA in

---

[13]The Euro values of ΔCoVaR is obtained by multiplying the original percentage values by the book values of equity.

Spain have high DIP, but were not identified as G-SIFI's.[14] So we may conclude that Italian and Spanish banks have become more systemically important, even though this may not yet have been fully appreciated by international regulators.

Figure 12 plots the DIP measure, based on senior and subordinated debt, in comparison to the SRisk measure based on 5% leverage ratio. All the measures rose during the two crises, but the DIP measures appear to capture the magnitude of the sovereign debt crisis more clearly. In particular, the DIP measure based on subordinated debt increases most significantly during the peak of 2011 than either of the other two measures do. It appears that the DIP measures incorporate the contribution of the sovereign risk premium more directly than SRisk.

4.4 DIP and bank-specific characteristics

In the previous sections we analyzed the evolution of DIP and its components at the aggregate and individual bank level over the past decade. We found a strong relationship between important events in the euro area and inflection points in DIP. However, from a policymaker's perspective, it is more relevant to assess which characteristics make banks more prone to contribute to systemic risk than to analyze real-time buildup in financial stress. Following Adrian and Brunnermeier (2011), we explore this question by testing the forecasting power of a group of accounting- and market-based bank-specific measures. We want to test whether these indicators are significantly correlated with the bank-specific DIP one and two years ahead.

Table 8 shows the results of a set of panel regressions where we use the yearly average of DIP (columns1-4) and the maximum value of DIP within a year (columns 5-7) as the dependent variables. All specifications are estimated with data between 2006 and 2013 and include bank-fixed effects and standard errors that are clustered at the bank level. Depending on the specific set of variables included in the estimations, the sample of banks varies between

---

[14]In the updated G-SIFI list published by the Financial Stability Board (FSB) on November 1, 2012, BBVA is included while Intesa Sanpaolo is not.

47 and 55 banks.

As expected, the coefficient on bank size, as measured by Log assets, is positive and significant in most specifications. By construction, DIP includes banks' size as one of its components. More important, we analyze the effect of banks asset structure on the systemic risk of banks. We use two proxies to capture the composition of assets: Loans/Assets and Liquid assets/Deposits and ST funds. The first measure reflects banks' focus on a more traditional lending business, while the second indicates the liquidity position of the bank. Both measures have negative and significant coefficients in all the specifications that use the one-year-ahead DIP. We interpret this result as evidence that more traditional lending-focused banks and banks with more liquid assets are less likely to increase systemic risk.

Next we check whether the banks' capital structure is important in predicting DIP. First, Loans/Deposits measures to what extent loans are financed with deposits, which are deemed to be a more stable source of financing. We find that the coefficient on this measure is positive and significant for the one-year-ahead DIP implying that banks that finance their lending with non-deposit instruments may be more prone to contribute to systemic risk in the short run. Second, we use Equity/Assets to capture the effect of the banks' book equity financing on systemic risk. We find a positive and significant coefficient for this variable across some of the specifications. This could potentially be explained by the risk-taking incentives described in Perotti, Ratnovski, and Vlahu (2011). Banks with more equity, potentially through regulatory requirements, may have the incentive to take on tail-risks leading to an increased systemic contribution when these risks are realized.

We also test for the predictive importance of bank profitability as measured by the return on average assets (ROA). The coefficient on this measure does not enter significantly in any of the specifications. In contrast, the Market to Book ratio, a market-based measure, appears to have an shifting correlation with DIP. Its coefficient is negative and significant in the one-year-ahead estimations and positive in the two-year-ahead specifications. Market prices are more volatile than accounting measures, thus, their relationship to systemic risk may also be unstable.

Lastly, we include a ratings-based measure of government support in columns 2, 4, 6, and 8 as an explanatory variable. This variable is computed as the difference, in ratings notches, between a bank's deposit rating and its standalone rating, as reported by Moody's Investor Services. This wedge between the two ratings reflects any potential external support, including support from the government, received by the bank. Given that the banks in our sample do not include subsidiaries of other banks, external support in this case reflects only systemic government support.[15] The coefficient on this variable is positive and significant in all specification. As explained in Brandao-Marques, Correa, and Sapriza (2013), banks with more government support are more likely to engage in risk-taking and contribute to systemic risk. Government support of banks reduces investors' incentive to discipline banks, allowing them to engage in risker activities.

5   Concluding remarks

As Europe has balanced on the edge of a second major financial crisis, concerns have mounted about the possible amplification of the crisis due to distress in the European banking system. Although banks may not have started the crisis in some of the troubled euro-area countries, as could be claimed for the global financial crisis, European banks pose significant systemic risk to the European economy. If a large systemically important European bank were to fail, or a systemically important group of small European banks were to fail, it would have dramatic implications in Europe and around the world.

In this paper, we build on the existing research on macroprudential regulation (Huang, Zhou, and Zhu, 2009; Adrian and Brunnermeier, 2011; Huang, Zhou, and Zhu, 2012; Acharya, Engle, and Richardson, 2012) to provide a systemic risk indicator that quantifies the risk of the European banking system. Our measure is a "distress insurance premium" that captures the cost of insuring the banking system against severe losses. Using market-based

---

[15]See Correa, Lee, Sapriza, and Suarez (2012) for more details on the construction of this variable.

prices, such as CDS spreads and equity correlations, and banks' liability sizes, we construct a forward-looking measure of each bank's systemic risk.

Our results show that the systemic risk of the European banking system reached its peak in November 2011 during the height of Europe's sovereign debt crisis. This points to the high stakes European leaders in wrestling with the downside risk of not resolving the crisis. Although increased risk premia were a significant component of this increased systemic risk, we also show that "physical" probabilities of default increased dramatically during this period. This suggests that the risk was not just due to changes in investor sentiment, but also due to real increases in the solvency risk of European banks.

We are also able to isolate the contributions of individual banks and groups of banks to the aggregate risk. We find that U.K. banks increased in systemic risk prior to the global financial crisis, consistent with their role as leaders in the global financial markets. Following the collapse of Lehman, the U.K. banks fell in importance and only gradually recovered over time. German banks, which took on significant exposure to U.S. subprime mortgage securities during the financial crisis, also declined in systemic importance following the height of the crisis.

The interesting story leading into the sovereign crisis is the Italian and Spanish banks. Although these banks were very minor players in terms of systemic risk prior to the crisis, the marginal contribution of these banks has grown significantly. When the systemic risk indicator reached its peak in 2011, these banks were significant contributors to risk in Europe. Interestingly, this is largely driven by the risk premia associated with these banks rather than the real probabilities of default. This suggests that the contagion concerns flowing from Greece to these countries was likely a significant component in driving up their systemic risk.

More importantly, we find that banks' economic fundamentals predict the one-year ahead systemic risk contributions of each banks, in an economically meaningful way. In particular, size and leverage forecast increases in systemic risk, while short-term liquidity adequacy and a favorable market valuation ratio forecast decreases in systemic risk. Interestingly, the traditional capital adequacy ratio and implicit government support actually lead to increases in systemic risk, which may be indicating that the old microprudential regulation regime gives banks incentives to take on more systemic risk.

The global financial crisis and the European sovereign debt crisis have caused policymakers to reconsider the institutional framework for overseeing the stability of their financial systems. It has become generally accepted that the traditional microprudential or firm-level approach to financial stability needs to be complemented with a system-wide macroprudential approach, i.e., to pay greater attention to individual institutions that are systemically important. Our results support the the claim that large, interconnected European banks pose systemic risk and should be subject to greater regulatory standards—a pan-European macroprudential regulation scheme.

References

Acharya, Viral, Robert Engle, and Matthew Richardson (2012), "Capital shortfall: A new approach to ranking and regulating systemic risks," *American Economic Review: Papers & Proceedings*, vol. 102, 59–64.

Acharya, Viral V. (2009), "A Theory of Systemic Risk and Design of Prudential Bank Regulation," *Journal of Financial Stability*, vol. 5, 224–255.

Acharya, Viral V., Lasse H. Pedersen, Thomas Philippon, and Matthew Richardson (2010), "Measuring systemic risk," Working Paper, NYU Stern Schook of Business.

Adrian, Tobias and Nina Boyarchenko (2012), "Intermediary leverage cycles and financial stability," Working Paper, Federal Reserve Bank of New York.

Adrian, Tobias and Markus Brunnermeier (2011), "CoVaR," Federal Reserve Bank of New York Staff Reports.

Allen, Franklin and Douglas Gale (1995), "A welfare comparison of intermediaries and financial markets in Germany and the US," *European Economic Review*, vol. 39, 179–209.

Altman, Edward and Vellore Kishore (1996), "Almost everything you want to know about recoveries on default bonds," *Financial Analysts Journal*, vol. 52, 57–64.

Andersen, Leif, Jakob Sidenius, and Susanta Basu (2003), "All your hedges in one basket," *Risk*, vol. 16, 67–72.

Basel Committee on Banking Supervision (2009), "Comprehensive responses to the global banking crisis," Press Release by the Basel Committee on Banking Supervision.

Bernanke, Ben S., Mark Gertler, and Simon Gilchrist (1998), "The financial accelerator in a quantitative business cycle framework," NBER Working Paper No. W6455.

Bisias, Dimitrios, Mark Flood, Andrew W. Lo, and Stavros Valavanis (2012), "A survey of systemic risk analytics," *Annual Review of Financial Economics*, vol. 4, 255–296.

Blanco, Roberto, Simon Brennan, and Ian W. March (2005), "An empirical analysis of the dynamic relationship between investment-grade bonds and credit default swaps," *Journal of Finance*, vol. 60, 2255–2281.

Bolton, Patrick and Olivier Jeanne (2011), "Sovereign default risk and bank fragility in financially integrated economies," *IMF Economic Review*, vol. 59, 162–194.

Borio, Claudio (2003), "Towards a macro-prudential framework for financial supervision and regulation?" BIS Working Papers.

Borio, Claudio (2011), "Rediscovering the macroeconomic roots of financial stability policy: journey, challenges and a way forward," BIS Working Papers.

Brandao-Marques, Luis, Ricardo Correa, and Horacio Sapriza (2013), "International evidence on government support and risk taking in the banking sector," IMF Working Paper WP/13/94.

Brownlees, Christian T. and Robert Engle (2012), "Volatility, correlation and tails for systemic risk measurement," Working Paper, NYU Stern School of Business.

Brunnermeier, Markus, Andrew Crockett, Charles Goodhart, Avinash Persaud, and Hyun Shin (2009), "The fundamental principles of financial regualtions," Geneva Reports on the World Economy.

Brunnermeier, Markus K. (2009), "Deciphering the 2007-08 liquidity and credit crunch," *Journal of Economic Perspectives*, vol. 23, 77–100.

Chen, Long, Pierre Collin-Dufresne, and Robert S. Goldstein (2009), "On the relation between credit spread puzzles and the equity premium Puzzle," *Review of Financial Studies*, vol. 22.

Correa, Ricardo, Kuan-Hui Lee, Horacio Sapriza, and Gustavo Suarez (2012), "Sovereign credit risk, banks' government support, and bank stock returns around the world," International Finance Discussion Papers No. 2012-1069.

Crockett, Andrew (2000), "Marrying the micro- and macro-prudential dimensions of financial stbility," Speech at the Eleventh International Conference of Banking Supervisors.

Crosbie, Peter and Jeffrey Bohn (2002), "Modeling default risk," *KMV White Paper*.

Duffie, Darrell (1999), "Credit swap valuation," *Financial Analysts Journal*, vol. 55, 73–87.

Forte, Santiago and Juan Ignacio Peña (2009), "Credit spreads: An empirical analysis on the informational content of stocks, bonds, and CDS," *Journal of Banking and Finance*, vol. 33, 2013–2025.

Glasserman, Paul (2005), "Measuing marginal risk contributions in credit portfolios," *Journal of Computational Finance*, vol. 9, 1–41.

Glassmerman, Paul and Jingyi Li (2005), "Importance sampling for portfolio credit risk," *Management Science*, vol. 51, 1643–1656.

Gordy, Michael B. (2003), "A risk-factor model foundation for ratings-based bank capital rules," *Journal of Financial Intermediation*, vol. 12, 199–232.

He, Zhiguo and Arvind Krishnamurthy (2012), "A macroeconomic framework for quantifying systemic risk," Working Paper, University of Chicago Graduate School of Business.

Huang, Xin, Hao Zhou, and Haibin Zhu (2009), "A framework for assessing the systemic risk of major financial institutions," *Journal of Banking and Finance*, vol. 33, 2036–2049.

Huang, Xin, Hao Zhou, and Haibin Zhu (2012), "Systemic risk contributions," *Journal of Financial Services Research*, vol. 42, 53–83.

Hull, John and Alan White (2004), "Valuation of a CDO and an n-th to default CDS without Monte Carlo simulation," *Journal of Derivatives*, vol. 12, 8–23.

Kim, Don, Mico Loretan, and Eli Remolona (2009), "Contagion and risk premia in the amplification of crisis: Evidence from Asian names in the CDS market," BIS Working Paper.

Kurth, Alexandre and Dirk Tasche (2003), "Credit risk contributions to value-at-risk and expected shortfall," *Risk*, vol. 16, 84–88.

Merton, Robert (1974), "On the pricing of corporate debt: The risk structure of interest rates," *Journal of Finance*, vol. 29, 449–470.

Moody's Investors Service (2009), "Moody's reviews European banks' subordinated, junior and Tier 3 debt for downgrade," Global Credit Research.

Norden, Lars and Wolf Wagner (2008), "Credit derivatives and loan pricing," *Journal of Banking and Finance*, vol. 32, 2560–2569.

Perotti, Enrico, Lev Ratnovski, and Razvan Vlahu (2011), "Capital regulation and tail tisk," IMF Working Paper WP/11/188.

Peterson, Mitchell (2009), "Estimating standard errors in finance panel data sets: Comparing approaches," *Review of Financial Studies*, vol. 22, 435–480.

Puzanova, Natalia and Klaus Düllmann (2013), "Systemic risk contributions: A credit portfolio approach," *Journal of Banking and Finance*, forthcoming.

Tang, Dragon Yongjun and Hong Yan (2008), "Liquidity, liquidity spillovers, and credit default swap spreads," Working Paper, University of Hong Kong.

Tarashev, Nikola, Claudio Borio, and Kostas Tsatsaronis (2009a), "Allocating systemic risk to individual institutions: Methodology and policy applications," BIS Working Papers.

Tarashev, Nikola, Claudio Borio, and Kostas Tsatsaronis (2009b), "The systemic importance of financial institutions," *BIS Quarterly Review*.

Tarashev, Nikola and Haibin Zhu (2008a), "The pricing of portfolio credit risk: Evidence from the credit derivatives market," *Journal of Fixed Income*, vol. 18, 5–24.

Tarashev, Nikola and Haibin Zhu (2008b), "Specification and calibration errors in measures of portfolio credit risk: The case of the ASRF model," *International Journal of Central Banking*, vol. 4, 129–174.

U.S. Congress (2010), "Dodd-Frank Wall Street reform and consumer protection act," Public Document H. R. 4173.

Vasicek, Oldrich A. (1991), "The limiting loan loss probability distribution," KMV Working Paper.

Appendix

A DIP computation

This appendix describes the steps to compute DIP.

1. Run HP-filter on the expected recovery rates of the banks in the portfolio. These recovery rates are reported along with the CDS spreads in Markit's CDS data. The expected loss given default (ELGD) is equal to one minus the filtered expected recovery rate for each bank.

2. Calculate risk-neutral PD's using CDS spreads and risk-free rates, according to Equations (1) and (2). Convert these annual PD's ($PD_{1,t}$) into the quarterly PD's ($PD_{0.25,t}$) for our one-quarter insurance contract as follows:

$$PD_{0.25,t} = 1 - (1 - PD_{1,t})^{0.25}$$

Back out the default thresholds from the quarterly PD's by inverting the Gaussian CDF.

3. Estimate the non-parametric correlation matrix Σ using past one year of daily equity returns. Due to the missing data problem, the correlation matrix is estimated element-by-element based on pair-wise correlations between equity returns. The matrix is updated weekly using the rolling-window of one year. These estimated raw correlation matrices are not guaranteed to be positive semi-definite, so the next three steps will use the factor structure to treat the raw correlation matrices and speed up the simulation at the same time.

4. For each week, start with three common factors. Following Andersen, Sidenius, and Basu (2003), set an initial value for the diagonal $F^{(i)}$ matrix, and perform principal component analysis (PCA) on $\Sigma - F^{(i)}$ to find the solution B to Equation (4). Calculate the new $F^{(i+1)}$ matrix according to Equation (5). If $F^{(i+1)}$ and $F^{(i)}$ are close enough (sum of squared differences less than a given threshold), we stop. Otherwise, use the new $F^{(i+1)}$ as the initial value and loop over the PCA on $\Sigma - F^{(i)}$ and Equation (5).

5. Calculate the pseudo-R^2 for the estimated B matrix, i.e. the cross-sectional variation in equity return correlations that is explained by the factor structure:

$$R^2 = 1 - \frac{Var[\text{lowtri}(\Sigma - BB')]}{Var[\text{lowtri}(\Sigma)]}, \qquad (8)$$

where "lowtri" picks out the lower triangular elements of the corresponding matrix.

6. Our targeted pseudo-R^2 is 95%. If the current value is below this target, repeat steps 4 and 5, increasing the number of common factors by one each time, until the pseudo-R^2 is at least 95%.

7. Using the ELGD from step 1, risk-neutral PD from step 2, and factor loading matrix B from steps 3 to 6, simulate the joint probability distribution of portfolio credit losses for each week. In the simulation, we assume LGD is stochastic and independent of PD. If ELGD estimated from step 1 is at least 0.5, we draw LGD from a symmetric triangular distribution with mean equal to ELGD and in the range of $[2 \times \text{ELGD} - 1, 1]$. If ELGD is less than 0.5, we draw LGD from an asymmetric triangular distribution with mode equal to ELGD and in the range of $[0, 1]$. The triangle distribution assumption is for computation convenience (Tarashev and Zhu, 2008b).

Because we are sampling rare events of systemic distresses, we use the portfolio importance sampling (IS) technique, as proposed by Glassmerman and Li (2005), to improve simulation efficiency and precision. We generate 500,000 simulations of bank returns according to Equation (3), shifting the mean of common factors due to IS, and compare them to the default thresholds calculated in step 2 to find default scenarios. For each default scenario, we run 100 simulations of LGD to compute the joint losses of banks. The portfolio loss is the sum of the joint bank losses, weighted by their liability sizes and adjusted by the likelihood ratio of the IS procedure. DIP (quarterly insurance premium) is equal to the average of the portfolio losses that exceed 10% of the portfolio value (i.e. sum of bank liabilities) over the simulation loops. To make our DIP value comparable in scale to other systemic risk measures, we multiply the quarterly insurance premium by four to convert it into the annual premium, and report the annual DIP in Section 4 of empirical findings.

B   Data sources and definitions

Our analysis uses data for the period between January 3, 2001 and January 24, 2013. The list of variables and their sources are:

1. The daily CDS spreads and the associated expected recovery rate for each financial institution are retrieved from Markit. The CDS quotes refer to 5-year contracts denominated in euros with a "modified-modified" (MM) restructuring clause for both

senior unsecured and subordinated debts. We use the last valid observation each week to construct weekly CDS data.

2. The weekly return correlations are calculated from daily equity data, provided by Datastream. We use equity return correlations to proxy asset return correlations, and calculate non-parametric historical correlations based on the past one year of daily arithmetic equity returns.

3. Financial variables.

   (a)

      (2) Risk-free rate. We use the daily 5-year implied swap rate to measure the risk-free rate. The swap rate is retrieved from Bloomberg.

      (3) Default risk premium. We use the daily BBB-AA spread to proxy the corporate default risk premium. The spread is equal to the yields of ten-year Euro-zone industrials rated BBB minus those rated AA+/AA, both of which are retrieved from Bloomberg.

      (4) Liquidity risk premium. We use the daily three-month Euro LIBOR/OIS spread to proxy the liquidity risk premium. The data is retrieved from Bloomberg.

      (5) Sovereign risk premium. We use the daily difference between Germany 10-year generic yield and the average of Spanish and Italian 10 year generic yields weighted by their quarterly GDP's, to proxy the peripheral European sovereign risk premium. All the sovereign yields are retrieved from Bloomberg.

4. Banks' balance sheet information, i.e., annual information of total assets and total liabilities for the banks in our sample, is available from Datastream.

5. The EDF data is provided by Moody's KMV. We use the 1-year horizon for EDF, and the data frequency gradually increased from monthly to daily in 2006.

6. The DTD data is available on the web site of Risk Management Institute at National University of Singapore.

7. The daily SRisk and CoVaR in million US dollars are kindly provided to us by Clara Vega. We translate them into million Euros by the Euro/USD exchange rates from Bloomberg. Rob Capellini at NYU V-Lab also provided us with similar data and helpful insights.